New Leaf Press

Dog Tired

A *Learning Adventure* in

PERSEVERANCE

MUSIC CREDITS
CREATOR AND PRODUCER: TONY SALERNO
ASSISTANT PRODUCER AND ARRANGER: DAREK DOWGIELEWICZ
ADDITIONAL ARRANGING: PIOTR DOWGIELEWICZ
SPECIAL THANKS TO: ANN THOMAS, MONA MARSHALL, AND RAY PORTER
SOLOISTS: CALLI DYE, JEFF GUNN, NATASHA SMITH, AND KINGS KIDS.
WRITER: MARK COLLIER

FOR INFORMATION WRITE:
NEW LEAF PRESS
P.O. BOX 726
GREEN FOREST, AR 72638

ISBN: 0-89221-605-0
LIBRARY OF CONGRESS CATALOG NUMBER:2004114889

PRINTED IN CHINA

Beeper barked loudly and wagged his brown tail
As Bill read the poster at Peggy's Pet Sales.
It read: "Puppy Contest! Enter Now. Don't Delay!"
So Beeper and Bill signed up right away.

"C'mon, Beeper boy! There is no time to waste!
We've got to start now or we won't win first place!"
They zipped through the town with their entry in hand,
Zooming up and down sidewalks like Olympians.

They raced through the town like two maniacs
Then zoomed in their front door and right out the back.
"Beeper, my boy, this is where you will train.
We will practice and practice come sunshine or rain.

I will teach you to sit. I will teach you to stand.
You must choose to obey each and every command.
You will run lots of laps. You will leap over logs!
I will turn you into one incredible dog!"

Beeper wagged his whole body. He danced on his toes.
He stood on his hind legs then spun on his nose.
"If you want to win you will have to work hard.
We'll start bright and early right here in the yard."

It was clear Beeper wanted to win this contest
And to be the top dog who was voted the best.
So they practiced until the moon filled the night sky,
Then Bill sang Beep to sleep with bedtime lullabies.

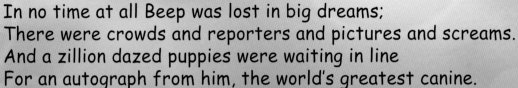

In no time at all Beep was lost in big dreams;
There were crowds and reporters and pictures and screams.
And a zillion dazed puppies were waiting in line
For an autograph from him, the world's greatest canine.

He pranced and paraded and
waved to the crowd.
He blew tons of kisses. He curtsied
and bowed.
Then as he stretched to take hold of
his prize,
A blast of bright sunshine beat down
on his eyes.

"Good morning! Good morning! Get up! Rise and shine!"
Bill sang as he lifted Beep's last window blind.
Beep yawned and he stretched and he stood to his feet
Then dashed out the door to prepare to compete.

"Good job, Beeper boy! Now,
    let's try some tricks.
First, jump through this hoop.
       Then, you'll fetch these two sticks."
Then just as little Bill blasted his whistle,
Beeper shot up like a rocket-launched missile.

"Wow, Beeper, my boy! You zipped through the ring!
You're great! You're tops! You're the jumping dog king!"
Then Bill grabbed a stick and reared back to throw,
Then he hurled that big stick just as far as it'd go.

"Fetch, boy!" Bill shouted and Beeper sped off,
Leaving thick clouds of dust making little Bill cough.
Then with the flair of a superstar hound,
Beep caught the big stick before it hit the ground!

"Double-wow!" Bill said dazzled, "Triple-wow!" Bill said stunned.
"My dog is a one-doggy-phenomenon!"
Bill hugged Beep and kissed Beep and tickled his tummy
And gave him four treats that made Beeper go "Yummy!"

"Okay, Beep," Bill motioned, "Come right over
    here.
Sit up straight. Look at me. And open both ears.
You've mastered the hoop jump. You're great
    with the sticks.
But now we must learn some amazing new tricks."

"The first one we'll do is real easy: shake hands."
Beep tilted his head trying to understand.
"Come on, Beep," Bill prodded. "You know, go like this."
Then Bill lifted Beeper's paw into his fist.

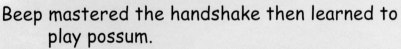

Beep mastered the handshake then learned to play possum.
His juggling routine is unquestionably awesome.
He does triple back flips on the trampoline,
And his spinning plates bit is the best one I've seen!

He learned the piano, the harp and guitar.
He can clog dance to "What a Good Cowboy I Are."
He can swallow long swords that are blazing with fire,
While standing on one foot upon the high wire.

He can roller skate backwards.
Blow bubbles with gum.

He can jump rope for hours.
Spin balls on his thumb.

He can paint. He can color. He
can eat with chopsticks.
For a dog he sure can do some
pretty cool tricks.

Little Bill taught Beeper to walk smooth and straight.
He stacked books on his head and then he stacked plates.
If Beeper walked too fast or bounced up and down,
The books and the plates would all crash to the ground.

They primped and they powdered.
    They combed and they scrubbed.
They ate only fat-free, protein-enriched grub.
They used "Puppy-Glow" so Beep's bod would look tanner.
Beep learned to bark "thank you" and other good manners.

There was no doubt that Beeper would win this contest.
He was better than good. He was better than best.
Then on Tuesday the weather had turned a bit cold
So they finished Beep's costume and put practice on hold.

Well, this is where things take a definite turn,
And where some big lessons will have to be learned.
You see, it snowed hard and soon covered the ground
And it didn't stop snowing till it hid the whole town!

Snow blocked all the windows. Snow jammed all the doors.
Snow covered the buildings and buried the stores.
No one went to school. No one wandered about.
No one could get in and no one could get out.

"Beeper! Wake up!" little Bill jumped and screamed,
"Our yard looks like a big bowl of ice cream!"
They both put on sweaters and turned up the heat
And wore two pair of socks to warm up their cold feet.

The fireplace crackled and made Beeper warm.
He reasoned, "Three days off will do me no harm."
Soon Beeper, all bundled up, toasty and snug
Stretched out a long yawn and curled up on the rug.

"Okay, Beeper, boy. This is no time to rest.
We still have to work to win the contest."
But Beep didn't care. He sprawled out on
    the floor.
Dug in his paws and then started to snore.

He slept in all morning, right up until noon,
Then plopped on the sofa and watched twelve cartoons.
He ate caramel popcorn, four boxes, at least,
Then bloated his tummy with a chocolate feast.

"Beeper," Bill pleaded, "Don't waste this whole day,
The Top Dog Contest is just three days away!"
Ha! Beeper mused, *little Bill should relax.*
I'll win this contest — that I know for a fact.

Ahh, this is the life, Beeper smiled and kicked back,
Watching the TV and popping down snacks.
Practice is fine but I've done far enough.
I'd much rather spend my time doing this stuff.

He stared at the TV till four in the morning,
Then slept with the bucket he'd had his popcorn in.
The next day his eyes were both puffy and red,
And his legs and his brain worked like they were half dead.

Bill was sore disappointed and a little perplexed.
Beeper slept all that day and then into the next.
Beeper had done what you never should do.
He had started a task and then not followed through.

Bill sighed, "I'm so sad things have turned out this way.
The Top Dog Contest is in just one more day.
Please listen, Beeper, if you choose to give up,
Believe me, you'll be one extremely sad pup."

And Bill was right. The sure way to feel good
Is to do all the things that you know that you should.
When you give up on something you'd like to achieve,
You lose all the good things you would have received.

All day the snow melted all over the town —
All the snow on the buildings and snow on the ground.
What a beautiful day for the dog competition —
The ultimate showcase for canine ambition.

Bill woke up excited and
destined for glory.
But Beeper, my friend, is a
whole different story.
It took him two hours to
climb out of bed!
He felt like molasses
inside of his head.

Beep's movements were sluggish. His muscles were sore.
His eyes didn't open as wide as before.
He had eaten and eaten without exercise —
And in the those three days Beep had tripled in size.

"C'mon, Beeper boy, we're gonna be late!"
Bill ran out the door and stood by the gate.
Beep puffed and heave-hoed his way to the door,
Then stopped for a moment to rest on the floor.

"What's happened?" Beep panted, "I'm worn out. I'm beat.
I'm finding it hard just to stand on my feet."
Beep put his chin down on his front paws to rest
And soon fell asleep and missed the contest.

When Beeper awakened he cried and he cried,
And just like Bill said he felt awful inside.
But he learned a big lesson that you could learn, too.
When you begin something always follow through.

Tony Salerno's

CHARACTER BUILDERS™

"Dog Tired"
Activity Book

A Learning Adventure in
PERSEVERANCE

By Katherine Vawter and David Sparks
Design and Illustration by M. G. Ron Johnson and Tim Davis

To the Parent/Leader/Teacher

This activity resource book features the story "Dog Tired (A Learning Adventure in Perseverance)" from the *Character Billders*™ series.

Little Bill's wild, wacky adventures teach valuable lessons in character building which are reinforced by the activities in this book. The fun-filled activities provide ways in which to apply the lessons learned to everyday situations.

This activity resource book contains lyrics to the songs from "Dog Tired." A variety of fun, simple formats are included for every age group. There are mazes, word puzzles, code breakers, and many more exciting activities that your child will enjoy. You may want to go over the character quality learned in each activity with your child. The activities may be completed individually or with a group. An answer key is in the back for your convenience.

Classic Entertainment™ hopes that the *Character Billders*™ series will encourage your child to develop good character qualities that will remain for a lifetime.

LEVEL OF DIFFICULTY

All of the activities in this book have been rated with three levels of difficulty for your convenience. You will be able to pull activities at a glance for the age group that you are working with. The easier activities are rated at one for younger children. Older children will be able to work the level three activities, but will also enjoy the less difficult activities.

You have permission to make copies — activity pages only.

easy   medium   difficult

Table of Contents

A Learning Adventure in
"DOG TIRED"
PERSEVERANCE

GET UP AND DO IT

Verse 1
Rise and shine, you sleepy head,
Rub your eyes, get out of bed.
We've got a full day ahead;
Let's get an early start.
Brush your teeth and tie your shoes,
Come on now, there's work to do.
We can't do it without you —
You're the most important part.

Chorus
Get up and do it. There's nothing to it,
You can get through it. Get up and do it.
Get up and do it. There's nothing to it,
You can get through it. Get up and do it. Get up and do it.

Verse 2
Now it's time to concentrate;
Working hard will make you great,
Do it now; don't hesitate;
There's no time to waste.
Every day you've got to train,
Through the snow and sleet and rain.
Build your body and your brain;
You're ready for the race.

Chorus
Chorus

© 1996 Angel Creek Music

SEE IT THROUGH TO THE END

Chorus

Whatever you start, see it through to the end.
You may never get the chance again.
So finish it, complete it, don't leave it undone;
Whatever you start, see it through to the end.

Verse 1

Maybe you're sailing the seven seas,
Washing dishes or raking leaves.
No matter what, don't ever quit,
Until you're done with it!

Chorus

Verse 2

Maybe you're training to run a race,
Or sending rockets to outer space.
Whatever job you have to do,
Make sure you follow through.

Chorus

You gotta be persistent;
You gotta persevere.
Someone who never gives up;
We need more people like that around here!

Chorus

Little Bill and Beeper sign up
for the puppy contest.

 36

PERSEVERANCE

MYSTERY WORDS

What should we do when we want to give up? Each word below has something to do with perseverance. Unscramble each word and write it in the square provided. The shaded column will spell out the mystery words.

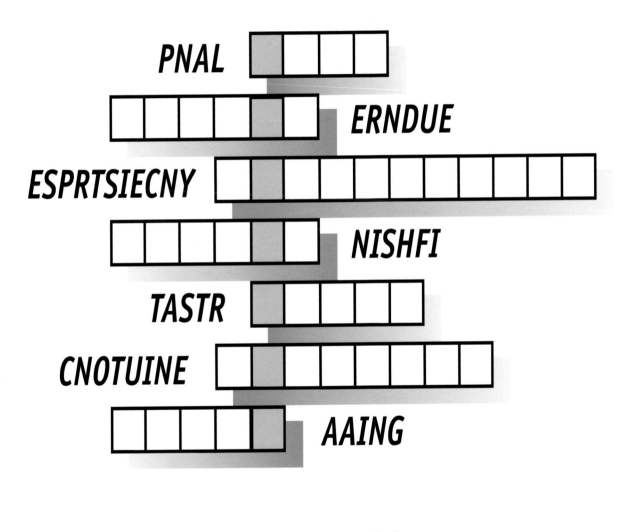

PNAL

ERNDUE

ESPRTSIECNY

NISHFI

TASTR

CNOTUINE

AAING

Write the mystery words here:

" ____ ____ ____   ____ ____ "

MYSTERY CODE

Use the mystery code to decipher the message about perseverance. Each symbol below stands for a letter in the alphabet. Match each symbol with a letter and copy it on the blanks.

⊕= A   ◆=F   ✓=K   ◈=P   ✳=U

▮ = B   ▢=G   ✪=L   ✌=Q   ✐=V

✎=C   ★=H   ✕=M   ✳=R   ◗=W

✔=D   ✍=I   ✛=N   ▲=S   ☞=X

☆=E   ⚲=J   ♥=O   ✖=T   ✿=Y

☛=Z

A L W A Y S

F O L L O W

T H R O U G H

_ _ _ _ _

Beeper dreams of being a winner.

FINISH THE PICTURE

Little Bill went to school before he could finish his drawing. He needs you to complete the drawing. Finish the drawing for him.

PERSEVERANCE

SOUND IT OUT

Use the pictures to sound out the words. Once you have sounded out the words, you will have a sentence about perseverance.

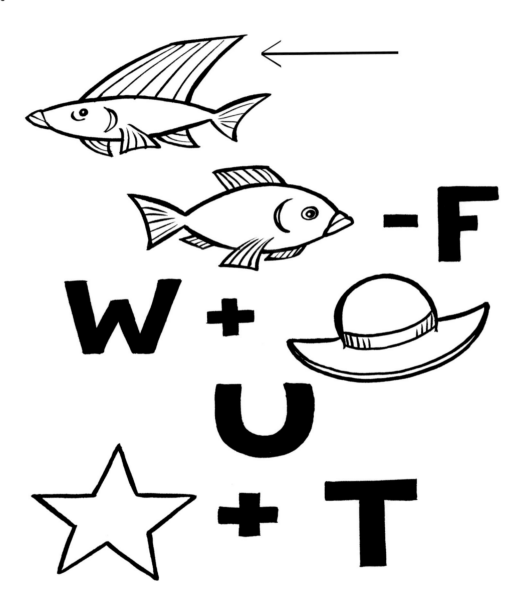

Write the sentence on the lines below.

_____

_____

Little Bill teaches Beeper some new tricks.

FILL IN THE BLANK

Work the puzzle by writing the names of the items in the blanks. Then copy the letters with arrows above them on the lines below. Make sure you finish this puzzle. Be persistent!

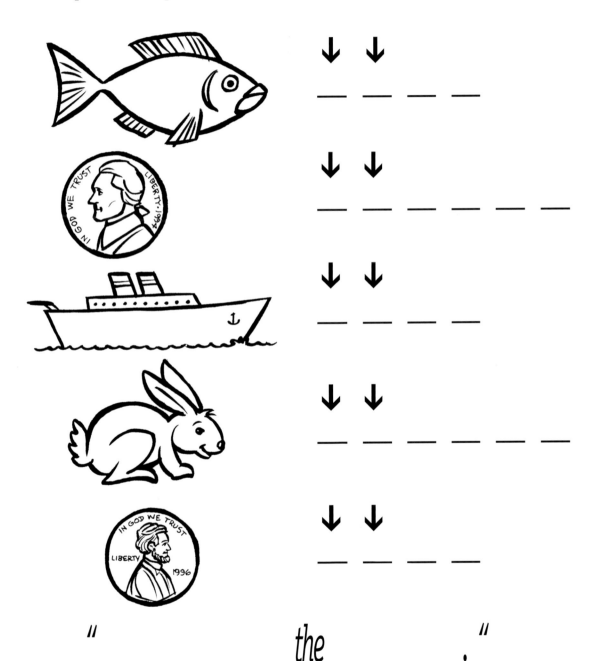

↓ ↓
___ ___ ___ ___

↓ ↓
___ ___ ___ ___ ___

↓ ↓
___ ___ ___ ___

↓ ↓
___ ___ ___ ___ ___ ___

↓ ↓
___ ___ ___ ___

" _ _ _ _ _ _ _ *the* _ _ _ _ _ . "

CROSSWORD

Write the correct word in the puzzle. The words are listed in the box below.

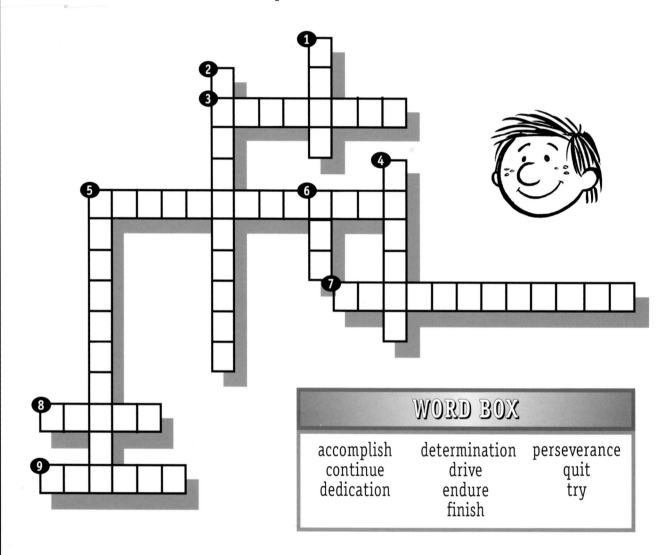

WORD BOX

accomplish	determination	perseverance
continue	drive	quit
dedication	endure	try
	finish	

ACROSS:

3. Keep going.
5. Beeper needed more of this.
7. When you decide not to stop.
8. Move forward.
9. Reach the end.

DOWN:

1. Stop.
2. Finish.
4. Stick to it.
5. Commitment.
6. Attempt.

44

"If I work hard, I'll win this contest!"

MYSTERY LETTERS

If you want to persevere, you must have another character quality to help you. Find the character quality in the puzzle below.

I'm a letter in MADE, but not in MAKE

I'm a letter in SET, but not in SIT

I'm a letter in TOOL, but not in POOL

I'm a letter in HERD, but not in HARD

I'm a letter in RAKE, but not in TAKE

I'm a letter in MOP, but not in HOP

I'm a letter in WIN, but not in WON

I'm a letter in BORN, but not in BORE

I'm a letter in MEAT, but not in MEET

I'm a letter in TAIL, but not in RAIL

I'm a letter in LIKE, but not in LAKE

I'm a letter in SON, but not in SUN

I'm a letter in NAP, but not in MAP

To persevere, I must have

— — — — — — — — — — — — — —

46

LETTER LEAP FROG

Circle the first letter in each line below, then skip two letters and circle the next one. Continue to do this until you have found the secret message. Then, write the secret message in the blanks below. Remember, don't give up!

(I)W(E)(F)ASAHNTUNFDNICNRHWSKITBDYPOOISU

(D)TNOWENKAOPETNYSLWUZSCOLCGMEEOEKFD

(T)HIRMEYCOTINRMAYSPADIGLEAZYIWLN

I F __ __ __ __ __ __ __ __ __ __ __ __

D __ __ __ __ __ __ __ __ __ __ __ __,

T __ __ __, __ __ __ __ __ __ __ __.

Beeper gives up and relaxes by the fire.

PERSEVERANCE

DOT-TO-DOT

Connect the dots and discover what the prize is for those who finish what they have begun.

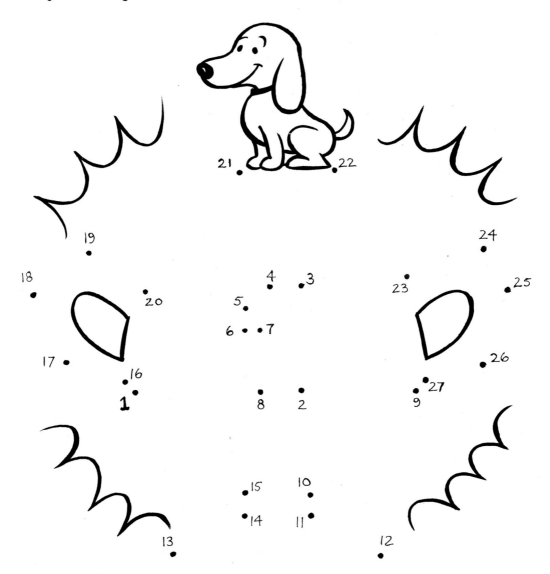

21 · · 22

19

24

18

4 · 3

23

25

20

5

6 · · 7

17 ·

16

26

1

8 · · 2

9 · 27

15 · · 10

14 · · 11

13

12

Have you ever run in a race?

———

How did you feel when you finished it?

_____

HIDDEN WORD

Find the hidden word in the rectangle by coloring all the boxes with a dot in them. For a real challenge, count all the rectangles. You can do it!

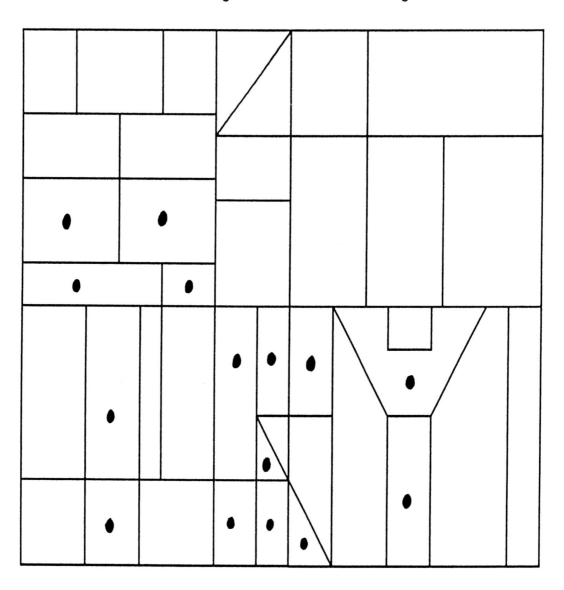

Write the Hidden Message here:

_____

PERSEVERANCE

Beeper did not persevere and missed the contest.

WORD SCRAMBLE

In the mountain of letters you will find the words in the box below. Circle each word. After you find them, can you make three sentences out of the words? Remember, don't give up!

```
                    R
                  B L A
                A M N O G
              M I T R Y P A
            T R Y E Y R E Y I
          S I E N R E M H P M N
        T G P R E       O M I G E
      B T H V D + + +   L U D R H
      E O E N E + + +   A P N T N
      T V B I N C       A M Q T A X
      Q M J R T H       N I O W A E
      L I K N I R T     H E Y L E I H
    X L O P T H Q       P H O R F N I
  C G E T N E V E R G I V E U P I T O R
```

AGAIN	EVERY	MOUNTAIN	TRY
CLIMB	GIVE	NEVER	TRY
			UP

Can you make three phrases from these words?

1. _____

2. _____

3. _____

PERSEVERANCE

MARATHON MAZE MADNESS

Beeper has started the race. Now help him finish it. You can do it!

Quitters never win and winners never quit. Quitters never quit.

Meet Quacker, little Bill's pet duck. Quacker is a good duck . . . most of the time. There are times, however, when he really wants to do something, and, even though he knows that he shouldn't, he just can't seem to resist. When Quacker does not control himself, trouble results. Little Bill told Quacker that if he can stay out of trouble, Bill will take him to the parade. Can Quacker restrain himself? Find out in this delightful adventure.

$14.99

ISBN 0-89221-604-2 • 60 pages • 8-1/2 x 11 • Hardcover

Little Bill is having trouble! Several of his items at school have disappeared, and his teacher, Ms. Beard, thinks he is losing his memory! After he visits a doctor, little Bill has to make some changes that cause him to be sad. The honesty of one student can make Bill's life happy again, but will the other student tell the truth? Find out in this fun adventure!

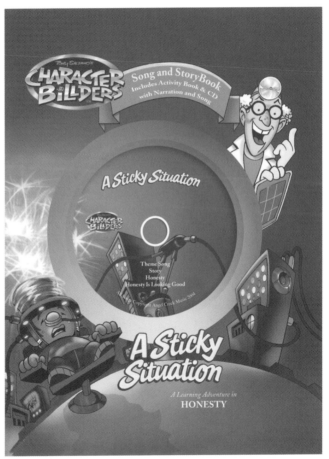

$14.99

ISBN 0-89221-606-9 • 60 pages • 8-1/2 x 11 • Hardcover

Where's Beeper?

Finding yourself lost in a strange place can be a scary experience. Little Bill and his puppy, Beeper, have become separated in a city where everything moves fast and the people are very busy — too busy, it seems, to help little Bill find his dog. By the end of this adventure, the people and Bill learn that life is best when you help others.

$14.99

ISBN 0-89221-603-4 • 60 pages • 8-1/2 x 11 • Hardcover

ANSWER KEY

MYSTERY WORDS - Page 37
"PRESS ON"

MYSTERY CODE - Page 38
"ALWAYS FOLLOW THROUGH"

FINISH THE PICTURE - Page 40

SOUND IT OUT - Page 41
"FINISH WHAT YOU START"

FILL IN THE BLANK - Page 43

FISH

NICKEL

SHIP

RABBIT

CENT

"FINISH THE RACE"

CROSSWORD - Page 44

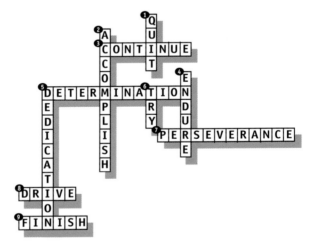

ANSWER KEY

MYSTERY LETTERS - Page 46
"DETERMINATION"

LETTER LEAP FROG - Page 47
*"IF AT FIRST YOU
DO NOT SUCCEED,
TRY, TRY AGAIN."*

DOT-TO-DOT - Page 49

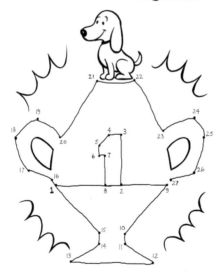

HIDDEN WORD - Page 50
"TRY"

WORD SCRAMBLE - Page 52

```
              R
             B L A
            A M N O G
          M I T R Y P A
          T R Y E Y R E Y I
         S I E N R E M H P M N
        T G P R E     O M I G E
        B T H V D + + + L U D R H
        E O E N E + + + A P N T N
       T V B I N C     A M O T A X
       Q M J R T H     N I O W A E
       L I K N I R T   H E Y L E I H
      X L O P T H Q     P H O R F N I
      C G E T N E V E R G I V E U P I T O R
```

NEVER GIVE UP
TRY, TRY AGAIN
CLIMB EVERY MOUNTAIN

MARATHON MADNESS MAZE
- Page 53

LITTLE BILL™ AWARD

Presented to

for successfully completing activities from
the Learning Adventures of
the **Character Bildders**™ series

"Dog Tired" about
PERSEVERANCE

Date

Tony Salerno